796.43

High Jump

ALSO BY DR. FRANK RYAN

Weight Training

THE VIKING LIBRARY OF SPORTS SKILLS

HIGH JUMP

DR. FRANK RYAN

NEW YORK / THE VIKING PRESS

Copyright © 1969 by Frank Ryan
All rights reserved

First published in 1969 by The Viking Press, Inc.
625 Madison Avenue, New York, N.Y. 10022

Published simultaneously in Canada by
The Macmillan Company of Canada Limited

Library of Congress catalog card number: 68-22869

Printed in U.S.A.

All illustrations by courtesy of Ryan Films, Inc. Copyright © 1960 by Ryan Films, Inc.

Second printing November 1971

Preface

In selecting the high jump, you have picked a fine and ancient event. No athletic activity can be more basic than "How high can you jump?" Even before the ancient Greeks men competed to see who could jump highest. Jumping is a basic part of many other sports.

This book was written to be as helpful as possible to you. It deals with the specific points of technique that make for good jumping, but, at the same time, constantly reminds you of the basic task. It also attempts to say something useful about the learning problems you are bound to encounter.

Not all of your questions will be answered by this book, nor will solutions be provided to all of the problems that arise. However, it is based on the experiences and beliefs of a host of famous coaches and successful jumpers.

It is not hard to get excited about jumping. We hope you will. Learning this classic event will be a rich and rewarding part of your life.

Contents

Preface	v
The Task	3
The Style You Will Use	6
Equipment	10
The Name of the Game Is "Height"	13
Clearing the Crossbar	25
Lead Leg	32
Strength and Condition	37
Getting Started	49
Your Coach	58
Learning	60

High Jump

The Task

As you learn the high jump, you will be working on specific points of technique. All these points of form will be easier to grasp and easier to master if you see them as part of a total picture. The parts will fit together and make much more sense to you.

Our model (photo sequence 1) allows us to see the basis of high jumping in simple form. Let the block of wood represent the jumper. We have put an **X** on the block to represent the jumper's center of gravity. The task is to get the block over the crossbar. To accomplish this the block's center of gravity must rise. The block is lifted until the **X** is higher than the crossbar. But this is still not enough for clearance. The crossbar is knocked down.

We now repeat the demonstration but with one difference (photo sequence 2). As before, the block is raised until the **X** is higher than the crossbar. But now the block is turned on its side. This allows clearance. The block can now pass over the crossbar.

The demonstration is simple but shows the basic task of the high jumper. He must both *lift* and *clear*. In other words he must get as much body height as he possibly can . . . and then clear the crossbar with efficiency.

An effective lift! An efficient clearance! These two points form the entire basis of good high jumping. The task is to get the body high in the air and then make the most of that body height by a good clearance.

In your career as a high jumper everything you do will have some relation to these two points. All your training and all your learning are related to attempts to increase lift and to improve the efficiency of clearance.

We will be working together on some specific points of technique, but these will be more meaningful and easier to learn if we keep the basic tasks in mind—LIFT and CLEAR.

1. The body must be raised, but lift alone is not enough.

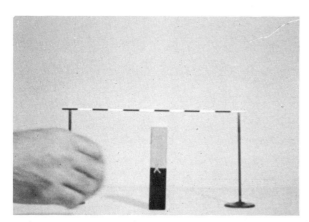
1a

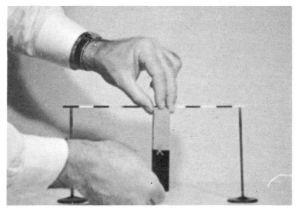
1b

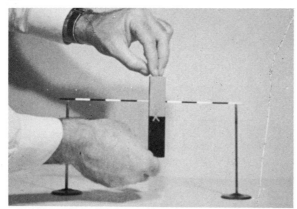
1c

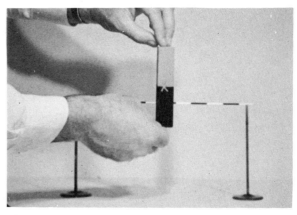
1d

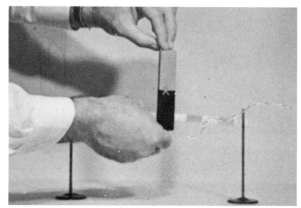
1e

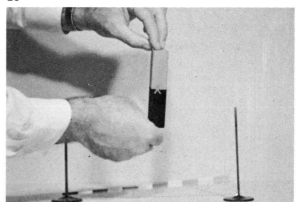
1f

2. It takes both lift and an efficient clearance.

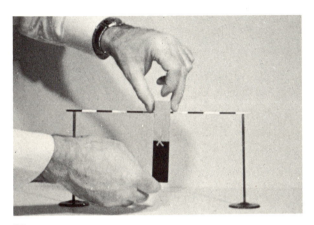
2a

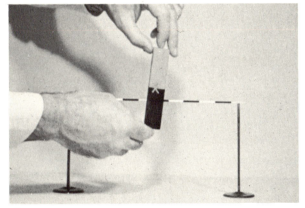
2b

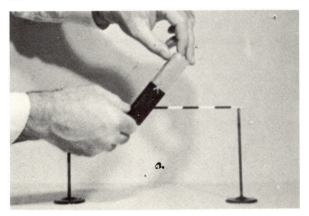
2c

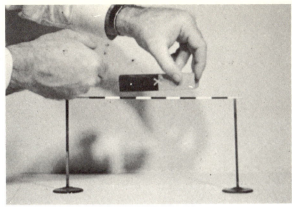
2d

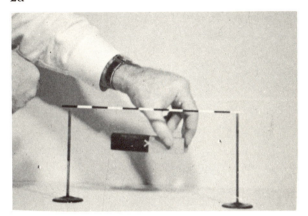
2e

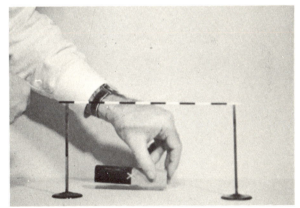
2f

The Style You Will Use

Not long ago nearly every book dealing with the high jump devoted a lot of space to discussing and comparing the various styles of jumping. The idea was that you could look them over and pick the one you liked. Today, these discussions are mostly of historical interest. The straddle, or belly roll, is clearly a more efficient way of clearing a crossbar than other styles used in the past. It is the style used by all of the world's great jumpers—with one extraordinary exception.

At the 1968 Olympic games in Mexico City, Dick Fosbury, the high-jump winner, showed a most unusual style of clearance. After take-off Fosbury turned his back to the crossbar. He cleared the bar on his back and landed in the pit on his back. Fosbury's great winning performance naturally caught the attention of coaches and jumpers all over the world. No doubt thousands of athletes are experimenting with the clearance style used so successfully and dramatically by Fosbury.

It remains to be seen whether this new method of clearance can and should be used by other jumpers, or if the style is an oddity suitable for one particular athlete. We may have an answer shortly. Meanwhile, however, it seems best to practice the straddle, a style that has produced so many seven-foot jumps and records.

In photo 3a the run, or approach, has just been completed, and the jumper is ready for his take-off. A long stride puts him into position to drive against the ground. The jump is made from the inside foot, or the foot nearer to the crossbar.

By 3d the jumper has done all that he can to lift his body. He is still rising. Now he turns his attention to clearing the crossbar. The object of the

The Style You Will Use

straddle roll is to make the best use of the body height that has been attained. It affords a better clearance than other styles.

The upper body, having reached its full height, is beginning to drop (3e). At the same time as the head and upper body begin to drop, another motion is under way. The body is rolling around the bar. The combination of the two movements raises the lower body, permitting it to clear the crossbar. The dropping and rolling motions are continued into the pit. Landing is on the lead leg and upper body.

You have had a quick look at the straddle style of jumping. This is the jump that we will be examining in detail.

3. Bob Gardner, a great stylist, shows the straddle form of jumping that we will be working with in this book.

3c

3a

3d

3b

3e

3f

3i

3g

3j

3h

Equipment

One of the great advantages of track and field is that the equipment can be simple. Fairly elaborate equipment has been introduced, but you don't need it to get started. Many champions started in their own back yards with equipment they put together themselves. Basically, what you need will be a uniform, shoes, a fairly reliable surface from which to jump, a crossbar, standards to hold the bar, and a soft place to land. Let's take a further look at these articles.

Uniform. If you are out for your school team, your uniform will probably be issued. Track uniforms don't have to be elaborate, but you do need a warm-up suit. Many materials, including wool and cotton, are satisfactory. Just make sure you wear it when it is cool.

Surfaces. You can practice from almost any kind of surface that will give you support. The best take-off surfaces are the newly invented all-weather materials. As the name indicates, they are reliable under all kinds of weather conditions. Even under constant use they remain solid and smooth. Eventually, nearly every school and college will have such surfaces.

In your jumping career, however, you will compete in many meets and may encounter a greater variety of surfaces. You may run into cinders, clay, soft wood, hard wood, commercial preparations—almost anything. Try to know in advance so that you can be ready. As for your early practice sessions, start with what you can get. Don't be fussy and wait for ideal conditions. At first, all you really need is a fairly level spot.

Shoes. Spiked shoes are permitted in some meets but not in others. Your coach will usually be informed in advance. If spikes are not allowed, then you will want to wear some sort of rubber-soled shoe that will give you

Equipment

traction. You can consult your coach or your local sporting-goods dealer. You need something that doesn't skid.

In most of your meets you will probably be permitted to wear spikes. Then your shoes will be similar to those used by the runners. The length of the spikes will be important. The length that is best will depend on the jumping surface. If the surface is of cinders or clay, the weather can make a difference. The wetter the surface, the longer the spikes. In general, the problem and its solution are easy to grasp. The spikes should be of such a length that they afford traction and can cut into the surface easily enough to permit the jumping foot to make full and solid contact with the ground. At take-off the spikes must be able to pull out of the surface without resistance.

Though many coaches prefer fixed spikes, this kind of shoe requires the jumper to own many pairs of shoes. Since spike length must vary with surface conditions, it seems better to have reversible spikes. Reversibles permit spikes of different lengths to be interchanged with the use of a simple wrench. The athlete can examine the surface that he is to use and then screw in the spikes of the right length.

After Charles Dumas made the first seven-foot jump and just before the John Thomas era, the Russians broke the world record with the controversial "built-up" shoes. This shoe helped them because it took advantage of certain physical principles. You may have heard stories of natives in Africa achieving remarkable heights, sometimes in excess of eight feet, by taking off from mounds. Of course, the mound itself is a big help in that it is higher than the surrounding ground. But much of the advantage comes from the slope of the mound—from the inclined plane that it presents. In jumping, much of the task is to convert forward motion to upward motion. Because of the physical principles involved it is easier to make this conversion from a slope than it is from a flat surface. The built-up shoe was an effort to build in the slope. As you would guess, the design of the Russian shoe was such that the heel was thin with the sole becoming increasingly thicker toward the toe. International rules now limit the thickness of the sole. Still it will benefit a jumper to wear a shoe on his take-off foot that will give him the maximum thickness that the rules permit.

Many jumpers are subject to heel bruises. Such injuries can interfere with practice. Protection for the heel is often needed, but this protection cannot be bulky, because it would make the lifting action less efficient. The best answer seems to be a plastic heel cup. It offers protection without bulk. The heel cup should fit well. If possible, it should be molded to the heel.

Equipment

Crossbar and standards. The specifications for this equipment are set in detail by the rules. When you are starting, however, don't worry about these specifications. You can practice with a bar that is not standard in either length or width. A piece of bamboo or any light wood will do. But do make sure that the supports for the crossbar are such that the bar can be knocked down easily. Never fasten the crossbar in place.

Pits. Homemade equipment can get you started. If you are out for the school team, a pit will probably be available to you. Take an interest in it and help maintain it. Take your turn with the shovel.

The purpose of a pit is to give you a soft landing. As you drop, gravity causes your body to build up downward speed. A good pit will help you lose that speed gradually, so that you don't get jarred by a sudden stop. Surprisingly, there was very little interest in pits until recently. Pits were made up of almost anything—dirt, sawdust, shavings, or sand. The introduction of rubber and plastics for pit fill has been a useful development. A school can buy these materials or, if it is lucky, get free scrap from a local factory.

The Name of the Game Is "Height"

In the term "high jump," the word "high" is all-important to you. Always keep that word in mind. You have to constantly think of height and lift. If you do, everything will come easier. More than ninety-five per cent of your work will be devoted to attaining sheer height. This includes your actual jumping and the training program that you will be carrying out.

Orientation. Athletes tend to be practical fellows who don't like hazy-sounding words. "Orientation" may sound like one of these words, but it isn't. It's important to you. You must be oriented *up*. As you work, you are going to be involved with various points of form. These points will have to be learned, but if you can get an "up" orientation, learning is going to be faster and surer.

Let's see if we can get some idea of orientation upward by following a great jumper (photo sequence 4). Looking at these photos you can almost feel that this athlete is thinking "up." In 4c and 4d the position of the head shows that his attention is directed toward getting height.

Contrast the photos you have just seen with photo sequence 5. You can tell that this jumper is not oriented toward height. Instead, he is oriented toward the crossbar—to getting by the bar and into the pit. His basic orientation makes it difficult to learn.

You will be getting on to the specific points of technique that make for good jumping. But all these points will be more meaningful and more easily learned if you keep thinking in terms of height.

Take-off. We will be coming back to the all-important subject of take-off. For the moment, however, take a look at some of the general points shown in photo 6. The take-off stride is being made. The jumper is in a good

The Name of the Game Is "Height"

position to make a long and powerful drive against the ground. He is ready to take advantage of a tremendous and effective power stroke. This is the key to fine jumping. Your run must culminate in a long, powerful, and fast push that lifts you high in the air. The take-off is the heart of the jump, and we will be returning to it constantly. But take another look at photo 6, and notice the length of the last stride and the leanback of the body.

Approach. The approach, or run, has only one purpose. It is meant to get you into an effective take-off position with momentum. The two key words are "position" and "momentum." Does it do it? There can be no other test.

When you observe the great jumpers, you will notice that they always approach at nearly the same angle. The angle made by the direction of the run and the crossbar is usually somewhere between thirty-five and forty degrees. If the angle were much smaller, the jumper would spend too much time riding along the crossbar instead of going over it. If the angle were much greater, he would not be in a good position to carry out an efficient clearance. He could not achieve the position almost parallel to the crossbar that is needed for straddle clearance.

Both the speed and the length of the run vary among the fine jumpers. A striking contrast was seen between John Thomas and Valery Brumel during their great duels. Brumel's run was much longer and very much faster than Thomas's. Brumel said that his fast run was made possible by his rigorous program of strength training. This is probably true in part, but there have been jumpers who used a similar approach and who had nothing like Brumel's great leg strength. A bigger factor was Brumel's excellent mastery of his event, which gave him confidence in his ability to reach a superb take-off position.

Certainly the run is one aspect of the jump in which the Russians have looked vastly superior in international competition. At the Olympic Games in Rome jumpers from other nations often appeared slow, hesitant, and unsure of themselves. The Russians contrasted sharply. They wasted no time in getting started, and they ran with speed and confidence, and without the slightest hesitation along the way. They were well schooled in this phase of the jump.

How fast should you run? Remember the purpose of the approach—to provide both position and momentum. If you were to attain excellent position but lacked momentum, you wouldn't be able to jump very high. In effect, you would be doing a standing high jump. On the other hand, great speed with poor position would not give you a chance to lift. In brief, you want to get the best combination of speed and position.

When you are first introduced to the high jump, the best combination of momentum and take-off position is produced by a relatively slow approach. As learning and training proceed, the speed of the approach can be gradually increased. Two things make this possible. The take-off pattern gets almost "built in" to the athlete's muscles and nerves, with a resulting increase in confidence. His training program gives him the strength to handle the added stress produced by the increased speed.

A very fast approach should not be artificially forced or developed too early in your career. It takes time and has to come gradually with increased learning and greater strength. But eventually you do have to develop a faster run. Your emphasis should be on controlled speed, the speed that you can control enough to carry out correct technique. A few fine athletes continued to perform with slow approaches throughout their entire careers despite their obvious ability to handle more speed. One wonders what they could have achieved. There had to be something wrong with their training routines.

Length of run and checkmarks. In general, a faster run has got to be a longer run. You need the extra distance to pick up speed. The great jumpers use as few as six strides and as many as ten. Most use seven, eight, nine, or ten. The typical successful jumper starts with two checkmarks. There is one at the beginning of the run and a second one along the way to give reassurance. With experience comes increased confidence, and after a while the second checkmark is discarded. The word "confidence" is important. To approach at fast speed you have to have confidence in your ability to carry out the jump when you arrive at the take-off spot. There are things to do when you get there. You have to be able to do them and know that you can. Practically anyone can carry out a fast series of steps and hit a target —provided there is no difficult task at the end of the line. But the technique of jumping requires training. If the training isn't there, the run is going to be slow and uncertain. In summary, there has to be a justified confidence in the take-off before there can be a fast run.

Direction. The run should always be straight. There should be no veering along the crossbar—no turning into it. At take-off, ideally, the jumping foot should be pointing directly along the line of approach. A few years ago it was observed that most of our best jumpers had a tendency to turn this foot inward so that it was pointing toward the pit. As a matter of fact, this foot position was so common that some of the experts began to teach this turning in of the foot as a desirable point of form. Later on, Brumel, among others, showed us what could be accomplished when the jumping foot was kept in alignment.

Oddly, the direction of the jumping foot should not receive direct attention by the coach or athlete. This direction is not subject to control. It is a symptom of how expert the jumper is. The average jumper has a strong and natural tendency to turn toward the bar before take-off. Even the very good jumpers share this tendency to a certain extent. It is part of an error of anticipation—the attempt to start the clearance before the take-off is made. Once this initial error is made, turning the jumping foot inward actually helps. It is a useful compensation for the error. Brumel had such a remarkably correct take-off that such compensation wasn't needed. He could keep his jumping foot in line with his run. In summary, the average jumper, and many very good ones, cannot avoid some turning in of the jumping foot. It is useless to try and change the placing of this foot. It will be more and more in line as the take-off improves.

Back to the take-off. Earlier in this section you were asked to take a look at photo 6. Your attention was directed to the power position, and it was suggested that you notice the length of the last stride and the leanback of the body. Both of these features are characteristic of the very fine jumper. The last stride is the longest of all. The vertical axis of the body is tilted backward toward the runway. Anytime that you see sequence photos of the champions you will notice the long last stride and the leanback. Also there, but less easily seen, is a settling of the hips. The take-off is really a power stroke. It takes power to lift the body high in the air. The stroke has to be full and fast, and made from a position that permits the use of the muscles. In short, the body's position has to be favorable for the application of power.

If you were trying to see how far you could throw a ball, you would want to apply all possible power. How would you go about it? Would you extend your arm forward and try for a short movement? Of course not! Before delivery you would lean your body toward the rear and draw your arm all the way back. Why? Because you know that you can get your best distance that way. Why is that? Because there is more time to accelerate the ball. There is a longer delivery or throwing motion. Remember the word "longer."

In any action the amount of power that is developed depends on the amount of force applied and the *time* during which that force is ap-

The Name of the Game Is "Height"

plied. Put another way, force by itself is not enough; there must be time to apply the force. Thus the take-off position must accomplish two things. It must give you both the chance and the time to apply that force. It must give you a chance to spring.

Nothing separates the average jumper from the champion so much as take-off position. The former's last stride is usually short, and he tends to topple toward the crossbar. He has very little chance to make an efficient application of power. His contact with the take-off area is brief, affording him very little time to drive. Even if he has a great deal of power in his legs, he won't get a chance to use it. The take-off stride of the champion is fast, but, even so, he gives the impression of a full-power stroke, that he is applying force over a long interval. In photo sequence 7 look especially at photo 7e. It is clear that force is being applied in a solid continuous way. There is still a backward lean of the body, even though the power drive has started. Application of power continues through to photo 7f.

Balance. Balance is necessary to power. Without balance you cannot develop force as you otherwise could. A simple demonstration will convince you of that. Have one of your friends do a squat. Now place your hands on his shoulders and try to hold him down. If he has average strength, you'll find that he will push right up through you. Have him squat again, but this time keep him slightly off balance. Now you can hold him down easily. His ability to exert force is greatly reduced when he is off balance. Jumping is an effort to exert force, so you can get a good idea of how poor balance can harm the jump. Balance when you are moving is somewhat different from balance when you are at rest. Yet the principle holds. You must be in balance to exert your best force.

The biggest cause of poor balance at take-off is the tendency to lean *toward* the crossbar instead of *away* from it. Compare photo 8 with photo 9a. In photo 8 the seven-footer seems to be driving almost straight up, whereas in photo 9a we can see a pronounced lean toward the bar. This lean is an anticipation of the clearance. There is an effort to get over the bar before the lift is finished.

The early lean toward the bar hurts the effectiveness of the jump in almost every way. It throws the jumper off balance and thus reduces the amount of force that he can apply. Because he is rushing forward, there is less time to apply force and therefore less power. In addition, the lean causes the body's center of gravity to be lower at the moment of take-off.

Let's return to the model we used earlier. Again, the **X** represents the center of gravity. With the body upright (photo 10a) before take-off, the body's center of gravity is at its closest to the crossbar. The drive at take-off has to raise the center of gravity enough to clear the crossbar. If the block is tilted to simulate the premature lean, it puts the **X** farther from the crossbar. This increased distance means that it takes more lift to get to the same place. The lean gives away valuable inches.

Improving the take-off. Again, remember that nearly everything you do in your training is intended to give you a more powerful take-off. All roads lead to a better take-off. Let's take a look at some of the roads.

We've already talked about orientation. But it is such an important point that we should emphasize it again. Your orientation toward the high jump is going to have an enormous influence on the rate at which you learn this event. If your idea of the high jump is crystal clear, if you constantly think in terms of "up," then it will be easier for points of form to fall into place. Your last stride will start getting longer. A leanback will begin to develop. Your lead leg is going to begin to whip up.

You will have to perfect specific points of technique, but your ability to master these points is going to be governed by your orientation. If your orientation is upward, it will be easier to learn these points. Athletes who lack the correct orientation never seem to learn to jump correctly.

For example, the leanback at take-off tends to come very naturally if the jumper is oriented toward height. Orientation is the basic framework. It makes all learning easier. The leanback is brought about by correct orientation, relaxation of the upper body, and leg drive. The essence of coordination is to work hard with one set of muscles and keep others relaxed. This takes training. The jumper who can drive hard with his legs on the last stride and, at the same time, keep his upper body loose is almost assured of good leanback. But this is a difficult task and one that can seldom be carried out perfectly. For this reason even the finest jumpers make a conscious effort to produce the leanback position.

Most world-class high jumpers try to drive the hips forward on the last stride. At the same time there is an effort to relax the upper body and let it drift back. There is almost the feeling that the legs are doing the work and running away from the upper body. The Russian coaches have advocated pushing this pattern a little further. They believe that the forward thrust of the hips should start sooner—on the next to the last stride. They feel that two strides can establish a better position than one stride. It is an interesting idea, but it is hard to know if any athlete has actually profited from such a two-step effort. It would seem difficult to execute this action smoothly and without interfering with running speed.

The Name of the Game Is "Height"

During your run, try to be leg conscious. (See photo sequence 11.) After all, the legs are the source of power, and they should have your attention. The last stride deserves special concentration, particularly the feel of the jumping foot against the ground. It will help if your "muscle memory" of the push becomes vivid. The foot moves into take-off position smoothly and without stamping, but the drive should give the feeling of being solid and firm. You should almost have the illusion that you are putting a full footprint in the take-off spot.

Correct action of the lead leg plays an important role in producing height. A full swing of the lead leg makes a direct and mechanical contribution to lift. It is a heavy part of the body, and getting it both high and moving at take-off produces greater body height. Good lead-leg action also helps indirectly in that it tends to bring about better balance. In another part of this book we will spend some time examining the use of the lead leg in detail.

To summarize this section, "Height is the name of the game." The most important goal is to get the body high in the air. Height is brought about by an effective take-off. Hence, the take-off is the heart of jumping. Developing a good take-off will occupy most of your practice time. It will be the main object of your strength and conditioning program. Learning to take off properly will not be easy. Your efforts at times are bound to seem frustrating and discouraging. Keep working! Keep thinking! When you finally have learned to carry out a reasonably good take-off, you will be on your way to being a high jumper.

4. (*a*) Approach. (*b*) Orientation is toward height. (*c*) Still thinking lift. (*d*) Attention toward lift. (*e*) Lift.

5. (*a*) Orientation is toward the crossbar. (*b*) A rush across the bar. (*c*) Not enough height.

6. Effective take-off position.

5*a*

7. A rhythmic run culminates in a solid position and a full-power stroke against the ground.

5*b*

7*a*

5*c*

7*b*

7c

7d

7e

7f

8. Balance permits a straight lift.

9. Poor balance means that less force can be applied.

9a

9b

9c

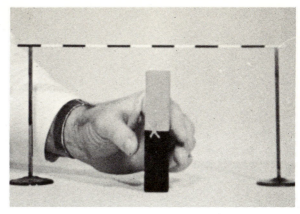

10a

10b

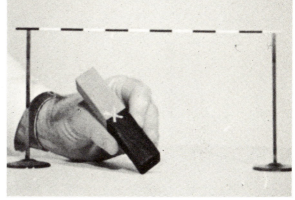

10c

10. A forward take-off lean loses valuable inches.

11. Attention is on legs! Legs! Legs!

11d

11a

11e

11b

11f

11c

Clearing the Crossbar

There is nothing mysterious about the straddle style of jumping. It simply provides the most efficient known method of clearing the crossbar. This style makes the best use of any given center of gravity height. In fact, when properly executed the straddle is efficient even with the body's center of gravity remaining *below* the crossbar.

We have already mentioned the two essentials of high jumping—lift and clearance. The first job is to get the body as high as possible and then clear the crossbar. The crux of good jumping is to keep separate the two main tasks, to do them in sequence—not together. First, the lift and then, and only then, the roll. The two parts should never be combined. After you learn to lift efficiently, it will be remarkably easy for you to learn a good roll. If you don't lift well, it is impossible to roll well.

In photo 12 the roll is efficient, but a sound take-off made this efficiency not only possible but easy. The jumper, already clear of the ground (photo 13), is still erect. He has "milked" a great deal from the take-off. Now that he is clear of the ground, the center of gravity's ultimate height and the path that it will follow are completely determined. Nothing can be done to change them. From this point on there is no way to harm the good result produced by the take-off. So full attention can now be turned to clearance. But only now.

Compare the photos you have just seen with photo 14. The poor clearance results from an early attempt to roll. The jumper tried to clear the bar before finishing his take-off. He failed to keep the jump and the roll separate from each other. In short, without a good take-off there can't be a good roll.

The two main features of the straddle clearance are (1) rotation of the body (the roll) around the crossbar and (2) a lowering of the upper body

Clearing the Crossbar

once it is on the safe side of the crossbar. These two actions will be examined. Carried out simultaneously, they produce a highly efficient clearance. But in all our discussion of clearance keep firmly in mind that the take-off is the important thing. A good take-off permits a good roll.

Let's look at the straddle style in some detail by following through a sequence of sixteen photos (John Thomas, photo sequence 15) of a jump in excess of seven feet. The approach is almost complete. Photo 15a shows a normal, comfortable, and balanced running stride. It is remarkable to consider that this is the next to the last stride. At this point the novice would be tense and rushing blindly toward the crossbar. The champion shows astonishing poise, in large part the result of his training. His upper body is relaxed, and he is ready for the critical events to take place during the take-off stride.

By photo 15b the take-off stride has begun. This great jumper's final stride is almost cobralike in speed, and yet he is able to hold form. The positions of the head and eyes tell you a lot about his orientation—it is UP! Photo 15d shows the long stride and extreme leanback so characteristic of the great performer. This is a picture to fix in your mind. Here is the base for the full-power stroke against the ground.

In photos 15e, 15f, and 15g powerful force is being applied. Two aspects are important. First, the time element. Force is being applied over a relatively long period of time. Remember that the total power you develop depends on both the amount of force applied and the time during which it is applied. The novice, because he destroys position by rushing forward, has very little time to apply any force. Second, the athlete is in a solid and balanced position. Notice, particularly in photo 15f, the firm and full contact of the jumping foot with the ground. This permits the application of great force.

The lead leg has been whipped up (photos 15e–15g) along the direction of the run. By photo 15h the right foot is already more than seven feet in the air. The full lead-leg action has helped both in lifting the athlete and putting him in a favorable position for the roll. The arms also have been driven upward. The contribution of the arm action is similar, but less powerful because the arms are lighter than the legs. Once the jumper has left the ground, all that he can do to promote body height has already been done. He can then turn his attention to clearance.

But in photo 15i he is still rising, and so far he has paid very little attention to clearance. This shows an excellent orientation toward getting height. Since the crossbar is more than seven feet, it means that the jumper's head and lead foot are more than *eight feet* in the air. What a base from which to carry out the roll!

The two main events of the straddle are beginning to take place. The head, having risen to full height, is now on the safe side of the bar and starting to drop. The lowering of the head and upper body helps raise the lower part of the body. At the same time, a turn has been initiated, and the athlete begins to roll around the crossbar.

For most jumpers the trailing leg is the great impediment. It is usually the part of the body that knocks off the crossbar. The novice spends enormous effort in a desperate struggle to get his trail leg out of the way. Rarely is this the case with the great jumper. Let's see what happens to the trail leg, but while we are looking at this action, keep in mind that it is made possible by the great take-off.

By photos 15k and 15l both the dropping of the upper body and rotation are underway. These two movements cause the trail leg both to rise and turn around the crossbar. By photo 15l the upper body has dropped more, and the rotation of the trail leg is further along. The key point is that the champion, unlike the average jumper, does not really have to work on trail-leg clearance. He doesn't have to give it direct attention. The mechanics of what he does take care of the clearance of this leg.

In photos 15m, 15n, and 15o the roll and the dropping action continue. By photo 15n the head is already lower than the feet. By photo 15o the head is approximately three feet lower than the trailing foot. The turn has progressed to the point where the athlete can look back at the runway. What has all this done for the trail leg? Take a look at photo 15o. The trail leg seems high enough to clear a height of about seven feet ten inches, so it isn't likely to cause much trouble.

The continued drop of the upper body is seen in photo 15p. The jumper's arm is already in the pit, while his trail foot is still higher than the crossbar. The rotation of the body is also continued. Many fine jumpers emphasize the rotation by continuing to roll right into the pit.

You have studied the two basic parts of the straddle clearance. Two motions are carried out at the same time for the purpose of getting the lower body clear of the crossbar. It looks simple and it is simple . . . provided you first get a good take-off.

The typical candidate has great trouble in clearing his trail leg. Jump after unsuccessful jump leaves him feeling frustrated because the trail leg seems to be the only problem. As a result, he tries emergency measures such as lifting the trail leg or trying desperately to kick it upward and out

Clearing the Crossbar

of the way of the crossbar. He isn't facing up to the basic cause of his trouble, which is that he has not learned to take off properly.

If any part of the roll, including the clearing of the trail leg, has to be rushed, it is wrong. The great jumper has the feeling of hovering. The roll can be carried out in a leisurely fashion. There seems to be more than enough time. By contrast, the beginner moves so fast and frantically through the perpendicular plane of the crossbar that he has no time to execute the basic movements of clearance. Of course, he doesn't have adequate body height in the first place, but to make matters worse he can't take advantage of the height that he does have.

Over and over again, the point has been made that mastery of the take-off must take place before a good clearance can be developed. Once you can lift well, you will have very little trouble learning the roll. Up until the time you have learned to take off efficiently, you cannot learn to clear efficiently. What does this mean in terms of your training procedure? The answer is simple. Put the bulk of your training time on developing a sound take-off, and for a while almost ignore the clearance. If you carry out your work with intelligence and determination, there will come days when you start hitting your take-off correctly. When that happens, you will know it by the hover feeling. Then the roll will be easy for you.

12

13

12.   13. A solid lift permits an efficient clearance.

14. A poor clearance because it started too soon.

15. John Thomas, an all-time great, demonstrates the straddle style at better than seven feet.

15a

15b

15f

15g

15h

15l

15m

15n

15c

15d

15e

15i

15j

15k

15o

15p

Lead Leg

All fine jumpers use a full swing of the lead leg at take-off. There are absolutely no exceptions. It is necessary to good performance. The evidence is so overwhelming that the candidate should need no special convincing. For one thing, we can look at the "empirical evidence." Don't be disturbed by this term. In this case it only means to take a look at the successful jumpers as compared with the poor ones. As mentioned, every good jumper has a full swing of the lead leg. Practically no poor jumper does.

In a moment we will be talking a little about the effects on lift of a moving lead leg. But even if there were no motion of this leg, the higher it is at take-off the better. The job in lifting is to raise the center of gravity. We want the center of gravity to be as high as possible at the moment of take-off. With the lead leg high in the air the center of gravity is higher.

Concerning the motion of the lead leg, you can carry out this simple but convincing demonstration (photo sequence 16). The athlete steps on a scale and notes his body weight (photo 16a). Now the lead leg is swung upward. The first result (photo 16b) is interesting—he actually becomes heavier. Note the position of the needle. But as the lead leg travels further upward (photo 16c), see what happens to the indicator. The athlete has become lighter. Remember, however, that the body weight is reduced only during the *last* part of the leg swing—not during the first part. Hence, the need for a very full swing.

You don't acquire a full lead swing right away and naturally. It takes practice. Even the champions give this leg action attention in their training. Photo sequence 17 shows one of the all-time greats carrying out one of his favorite and, in his opinion, most useful drills. He calls these exercises "jump-ups." There is no intention of making a full jump or of clearing the crossbar. The athlete is free to concentrate on and improve the swing of the lead leg. He doesn't have to worry about the rest of the jump. This champion and his coach say that the goal of this drill is to improve the lead-leg action to the point where the leg can swing directly overhead. Such a goal might not be reached, but the effort to reach it makes for a valuable part of the training routine.

By now you are probably pretty well convinced that you are going to develop a full lead-leg swing. From here on it will be mostly a matter of giving it enough attention in your workout routine. But your clear understanding of the need for a full swing is an important starting place. Most jumpers seem to feel it is enough merely to place the lead leg over the crossbar. The champion swings the lead leg about as high as he can.

In what *direction* should the lead leg swing? The answer is easy—right along the direction of your approach or run. The leg rises in line with the way you are moving. The average jumper almost always turns the lead leg in toward the crossbar. The champion swings it in line with the direction of his run. But in mastering this action he has overcome a natural tendency to turn the leg toward the crossbar. It took some work.

Should the lead leg be *straight* during the full swing? The answer has to be qualified a little. From a strictly theoretical viewpoint the straighter the leg, the more effective its action will be. However, the beginner cannot count on developing a straight leg swing and should not worry about it. In the beginning it will seem much more natural to flex the lead leg. With continued practice and increased confidence the lead leg will become more relaxed. When this happens the leg will gradually become straighter during the swing. Don't hurry this aspect of the jump.

The development of a full lead-leg swing has another important effect on your jumping. You cannot make a full swing of the lead leg unless you are balanced over the jumping foot. Constant practice of the lead-leg action will greatly improve your balance, and, of course, the better the balance the more force against the ground at take-off.

When you practice lead-leg action, there is a simple but important point to remember. This action eventually means a big improvement in performance, but you still have to spring from your jumping leg. You can't simply pull yourself up in the air with the lead leg alone. Usually when an athlete turns his attention to lead-leg action, he finds that his performance suffers temporarily. It's because he gets distracted and forgets to spring. This won't last long. Keep working on that lead leg.

The more limber you become, the easier it will be to get a full swing of

Lead Leg

the lead leg. Hence, your workout program should include exercises that will increase flexibility. The "jump-ups" will remain important. Even the champs continue to use them.

An upward swing of the *arms* at take-off has an effect on height attained similar to that of the lead-leg action. This point has probably occurred to you. Yet experience has shown that it is not a good idea for the beginner to spend much time on the arm action. Special attention to the arms and efforts to control them seem to interfere with the timing of the jump. As orientation becomes more and more "up," the arms should tend to move correctly. If they don't, there will be time enough to take corrective action.

16a

16b

16c

16. (*a*) Body weight. (*b*) Heavier with partial lift. (*c*) Lighter with fuller lift.

17. Even the champs practice lead-leg action.

17a

17b

17c

17d

17e

17f

Strength and Condition

Not long ago high jumpers did very little work. They were a sheltered group and avoided most activities, particularly anything that looked like hard work. Nearly everyone, including the experts, went along with this view. In those days a typical workout for a high jumper was somewhat as follows. After a brief warm-up, the athlete would run a little, stretch a bit, and perhaps do some light calisthenics. Then, he might do some jumping—but usually not much of it, because he had to "keep his spring." Those were the days when any jumper who could clear six feet was a very valuable member of a college track team. The Olympic record was six feet eight inches. Now the qualifying height for a high jumper even to *enter* the Olympic Games is seven feet.

The great advance in high-jumping performance has been paralleled by similar advancements in all sports activities. Over the last generation there have been improvements in both techniques and equipment, and certainly these improvements have played a part in the great advances that have been made. But the great common denominator in the remarkable avalanche of record breaking has been *work*. It took a while to overcome superstitions about "being burnt out," but coaches and athletes gradually discovered that the key to "impossible" performances lay in work, work, and more work.

Today, and in almost every athletic event, the athlete does double or triple the amount of work that was carried out a generation ago. For example, the great distance runners now carry out training schedules that would once have been regarded as suicidal. Weight throwers now have weight-training programs that were once used only by professional strongmen. But nowhere has the change been more striking or unexpected than in the high jump.

Strength and Condition

The evidence now is absolutely conclusive. You have to make up your mind that you are going to carry out a full strength-building and conditioning program.

Warm-up. Every day's practice must begin with a warm-up. The serious athlete never regards his warm-up as an unimportant preliminary—something to be gotten out of the way. He knows that the warm-up is more than simply a preparation for a session of jumping. He sees it as a necessary part of his entire conditioning program.

Your warm-ups don't always have to be the same. There are many things that you can do, and there are countless variations of these activities. The main point is to be sure that you do enough of them and establish the routine of a full warm-up.

The principal parts of your warm-up will be jogging, running, walking, hurdling, stretching, and calisthenics (photos 18 and 19 and photo sequence 20). With some amount of trial and error and with the help of your coach you will discover the routines that fit you best. You can experiment with a great amount of variation. But you should devote at least twenty minutes to your warm-up. Just as the term indicates, you should feel "warm." You should feel that the blood is circulating through your muscles. If you are on a school team, you will find that the coach expects you to have completed your warm-up before reporting for instructions.

Weight training. The introduction of weight training, more than any other single factor, has been responsible for the enormous improvements made in all branches of athletics. Today, weight training has spread to nearly all sports. There are many athletic events in which *every* outstanding performer trains with weights. It has become physically impossible for an athlete to make it to the top without a weight-training program. This situation is almost true for the high jump, and it will no doubt be completely true very soon.

Performance in most sports requires the output of power. The greater the power, the greater the performance. Certainly the high jump is a power event. With additional power at your disposal you can jump higher.

Let's follow the action of the take-off leg during a jump (photo sequence 21). A lengthened stride (photo 21a) brings the jumper into an effective position that permits a long drive against the ground. Notice the solid and balanced position (photo 21c). The athlete is right in the middle of his power stroke. In photo 21d we see that the leg is still partially bent. By photo 21e the leg has vigorously straightened out, supplying a great burst of energy for the lift. The straightening of the leg is the main source of power. Now this ability of the leg to strengthen with great force is not mysterious. There are muscles that do it by contracting. In this case the significant muscle is located in the thigh and is called the quadriceps. The stronger this muscle becomes, the greater the power it can supply and the higher you go. Now, of course, you can see the need to strengthen this muscle.

Squats and the leg-press machine. Jumping itself will develop the leg muscles to a certain extent, as will running, walking, and many other activities. But muscles respond only to the amount of work given to them. If muscles are to develop fast and fully they must be overloaded—that is, given much more work than they would ordinarily get. Weight-training exercises provide a means of controlling the amount of work that the muscles must do.

In general, when a weight-training program is designed for any athletic event, an effort is made to match the muscles emphasized by the event with specific exercises that will develop those muscles. In the high jump we know that we want weight-training exercises which will strengthen the muscles that straighten the leg. Two exercises that accomplish this are leg pressing and squats.

The champion you see (photo 22) working on the leg-press machine attributes much of his success to this activity. Such a machine is really a simple device. It can be almost any kind of *safe* gadget that permits a bar with its weights to slide up and down. The word "safe," however, is important. Have your coach or some other expert examine your machine for safety. You will be pressing a considerable amount of weight, and you must be sure that such loads can be handled without danger.

You will recall the old knee-bends that you did in gym class when you were in grade school. Well, squats are simply knee-bends with some weight on your shoulders. Squats are classified as full, one-half, or one-quarter, depending on how much you bend your knees. Most trainers and athletic coaches feel that it is best to avoid working with full squats, or very deep knee-bends. This opinion is based on experience, research, and reasons involving the structure of the knee.

When you carry out squats you will have a barbell resting across your shoulders and touching the back of your neck. The barbell will be kept in place with your hands. As you progress and the weights become heavier, you will need some protection to prevent the bar from biting into your neck and shoulders. The bar can be wrapped in a towel or other protective material.

Strength and Condition

The weights that you will eventually use for squats will be too heavy for you to handle with your arms. For this reason the weight is taken from a rack. In addition, it is a good idea to have teammates on hand to give you some help if the weight gets hard to handle.

What weight training does. Within certain limits and given enough time, your body has an amazing ability to adjust to the situation that confronts it. For example, the body can build up immunity against a certain type of germ if given a reasonable chance to do so. If the right doses of vaccine are administered, antibodies are created that protect the body. But the body could be overwhelmed if too much vaccine were given too quickly. The doses have to be correct to give the body its best chance.

The great Emil Zatopek dramatized the effects of hard work on distance running. In 1952 he won the 5000 meters at the Olympic Games with a startling time of fourteen minutes six seconds. Coaches discovered that his training schedule was more strenuous than anyone had thought possible. Today, Zatopek's time would be sixteen seconds too slow even to qualify him for the Games. Training schedules have become even more strenuous. The distance runner's body has been gradually and progressively trained to the point where it can tolerate a rapid pace for long distances. The heart muscle and circulation become very much more developed than those of nonrunners. How is it done? By work—systematic and progressive work. With increasingly severe running schedules the body becomes confronted with an increasingly difficult task. Just as in the administration of a vaccine, if the "right doses" are given, the body responds, and it becomes more and more efficient.

In short, the answer lies in subjecting the body to increasing amounts of work. If this is done in a planned and intelligent way, the body makes changes so that it can handle the increased load.

So it is with weight training. The body attempts to respond to what it is regularly called upon to do. If in your day-to-day living your body is not called upon to carry out acts of strength, it has no reason to grow strong. It then tends to stay about the same. If, on the other hand, your body is regularly required to do things that need strength, it will get stronger. But it needs a chance to adjust. The body cannot change right away. That's why you must be systematic and intelligent in your approach. You will be running into the phrase "progressive resistance." It means that you start off with a certain amount of work and then gradually increase the workload as the body gets used to it.

"Reps" and sets. Two of the common terms used in weight training may

already be familiar to you. "Reps," or repetitions, simply means the number of times you carry out an exercise without stopping. For example, if you raise a barbell ten times without pausing, you have done ten "reps." We can say that you have carried out one set of ten reps. If you repeat this procedure twice more, you will have done three sets of ten reps. These simple terms, "reps" and "sets," are used in describing all weight-training programs. You will hear them a lot in the future.

Exercises. Weight training has borrowed from weight lifting, which is a competitive sport in its own right. There are three formal lifts used in international competition. These are the press, the snatch, and the clean and jerk. Though these three competitive lifts are often included in weight-training programs, a great many other exercises have been developed. The list is very long. These many exercises have been invented by athletes, coaches, and other experts to meet special needs.

The procedure in devising and selecting weight-lifting exercises has been pretty much as follows. An anlysis is made of a particular athletic event. An effort is made to find out which muscles play an important part in carrying out that event. Then exercises are selected or invented to emphasize those particular muscles. The word "emphasize" is used because most athletic activities involve all or nearly all of the muscles of the body. It becomes a matter of which muscles seem to be the most important in producing performance.

Weight training entered the athletic picture against stubborn opposition. Most coaches fought the use of weights. The phrase "muscle-bound" was popular then. We know now that this phrase is meaningless. When records started to tumble in spectacular fashion, it was found that the new record holders, especially those in the field events, had been training with weights. It became clear that the proof was there. Everyone had to accept the value of weight training.

The once "delicate" high jumpers began to profit from leg pressing and squats. John Thomas devoted a good portion of his training time to the leg-press machine. The increased power that he developed helped him set a new world record. Other jumpers followed the example, and the level of performance went up everywhere.

John's world record was broken by the phenomenal Valery Brumel, who at a height of six feet one inch jumped more than sixteen inches above his own head. His strenuous weight-training program had included not only squats but a great range of other exercises. The contrast in physique between Brumel and the old-time jumpers was startling. This compact, power-

Strength and Condition

ful young man looked very different from the "beanpoles" who dominated the high jump a generation ago. Valery had so much all-round power that he could put the sixteen-pound shot over fifty-one feet, even though he gave this event very little attention. In summary, we had earlier evidence that leg pressing and squats could improve high jumping. Brumel's career taught us a further lesson. General strength and good conditioning are needed for top performance. Though leg exercises remain the most important ones, we now know that the jumper can achieve even greater performance by strengthening his entire body.

Your program. It's going to take trial and error to find the best program for you. As time goes by and you gain more experience, you and your coach will make changes in your routine. There is seldom a single program that fits all athletes. Your own program should be "tailor-made." What sorts of programs are possible? There is an almost bewildering number of possibilities, but don't let that disturb you. Picking your starting program from all the many combinations won't be as difficult as it might seem. You will have to select exercises, decide on the reps and sets to use, and then find the appropriate starting poundages.

The principal exercises used by the great jumpers include:

> Leg presses
> Squats
> Jump squats
> Toe-raises
> Dead lifts
> Pullovers
> Presses
> Leg lunges
> Bench presses
> Curls
> Sit-ups

In addition to these weight-training exercises performed with barbells and dumbbells, there are others performed with iron boots and various types of apparatus.

Once the starting exercises have been selected, you will decide on the numbers of reps and sets. In general, during the early stages the body has a better chance to make a preliminary adjustment if the weights are relatively light and there are many reps. Later on, you will have training days calling for fewer reps and heavier poundages.

Strength and Condition

When you start, the correct poundage has to be discovered. This is very easy to do. A little trial and error will quickly let you know how much weight you can start with and still be able to carry out the program that has been planned.

As your workouts progress, you will gradually and systematically increase the work load. Increasing the amount of work you are doing can be carried out in a number of ways, since there are three basic factors. You can increase the number of repetitions, the number or sets, or the poundage. Often, a combination of all three is used. For example, you might be able to carry out three sets of eight reps in a certain exercise. As you get stronger, you may find that you can do three sets of twelve reps. At this point, you might increase the poundage until you are back to doing sets of eight reps. You will then work up to sets of twelve reps. With still greater strength you can repeat the pattern.

How often should you lift? More often than you think, because weight training is going to be a substantial part of your program. According to a report by his coach, Brumel spent twenty-five per cent of his training time in lifting. Most fine jumpers lift three times each week. There is nothing magical about this number, but it seems to work out well. As you would expect, weight training during the off season is more intensive. When the weights were first introduced as a training method for jumping, most athletes stopped lifting entirely once the competitive season got underway. Not so today. Even when competition starts, weight-training is continued, though it is reduced somewhat. Some athletes continue to lift once each week and others twice. If competition is on Saturday, Wednesday is usually the last day of the week for weight training.

Weights attached to the body. At the Olympic Games in Rome in 1960, the Russian jumpers surprised the world and shocked the United States. John Thomas, then the world-record holder and the favorite to win, was defeated by two Russian jumpers and tied by a third. Robert Shavlakadze, the winner, and Brumel, who placed second, both cleared seven feet one inch. Bolshov made seven feet to tie Thomas.

Coaches and athletes clamored to find out about the "secret" methods used by the Russians. They found out, of course, that the Russian jumpers had done an enormous amount of work. These athletes had undergone rigorous strength and conditioning programs including weight training and much jumping—each jumper made as many as a thousand jumps in a single month.

The Americans were already familiar with the need for hard work.

Strength and Condition

What did seem new, however, was the Russian claim that much of their jumping was carried out with weights attached to various parts of their bodies. Their coach wrote that the attached weights were used to "reinforce jumping strength." Impressed by the Russian success, many American coaches urged their jumpers to work with attached weights.

It is hard to argue with success, but there are reasons to believe that attaching the weights is not a good idea. There are strong theoretical reasons for thinking that this training method can actually interfere with learning. We won't go into such reasons in detail, but attached weights make the high jump a slightly different event. The timing becomes different. It is probably true that the use of attached weights does build strength, but there are other ways of building strength—ways that don't interfere with the learning process.

Running. Running should always be included as an essential part of your training program. You can set up your running program in a way similar to your weight-training program. There is, however, one significant difference. Weight training seems to yield its best results on the basis of three days a week, whereas you can and should run every day.

Jogging will be important, especially in your warm-ups, but your emphasis will be on speed over shorter distances. Sprinting actually amounts to a series of power drives. The longer the distance that you run, the more the reps. In a similar way, the faster you run the greater the resistance—hence, the "heavier the poundage." In a true sense, running a short distance at top speed is like doing a few reps with a heavy weight; running a longer distance at slower speed is like doing many reps with lighter weights.

Since the high jump is a power event, even though the running program starts with longer runs at slow speeds, you will work toward shorter runs at faster speeds. You will do your running in "sets," though the runners will call them "repeats." As you work your way down to shorter distances at a faster pace, you and your coach may decide on "sets" of one hundred yards, seventy yards, or fifty yards. With increased conditioning both distances and the number of repeats can be changed.

Jumping itself. Never forget that you are a high jumper. Don't get so involved in building your strength and developing your conditioning that you lose track of your goal. Jump and jump often. Many candidates want to "save their spring." It is true that after several consecutive days of hard jumping you may feel that you have less spring. But two days' rest before the meet brings you right back—more than right back. You will have more spring than ever.

Training habits. If this book had been written some time ago, it might have observed the tradition of the time and said a lot about the harmful effects of smoking and alcohol. You would have heard a lot about adequate sleep and proper diet. Even now you might find it curious that so little is said about these topics. The answer is simple. If you are a serious and determined athlete, these things will not be problems for you. You will, as a matter of intelligence, observe good training rules. The great athlete does not have to be disciplined or coaxed concerning training rules. He is not fool enough to put himself at a disadvantage. He does not want to undo the hard work that he has invested in himself and his event.

18. High jumpers are no longer a sheltered group.

19. Running is part of every work-out.

20a

20b

20c

20. The warm-up is never neglected.

21. (*a*) A long stride into power position. (*b*) Power starts. (*c*) The bent jumping leg is straightening. (*d*) Force applied against the ground continues. (*e*) The power stroke is almost complete. (*f*) Lift! The result of force well applied.

21*a*

21*b*

21*c*

21*d*

21*e*

21*f*

22. Leg presses strengthen jumping muscles.

Getting Started

Let's assume that by now your conditioning program has been underway. You have been carrying out various exercises, including calisthenics, weight training, and running. Later on, you will be stronger and in better condition, but you don't have to wait until then to start jumping.

You may already be able to execute a fairly good straddle jump. If so you have a base from which to work, and the job becomes that of improving your present jump.

But if you've never done a straddle and want to get started, a good procedure is as follows. Three simple stages are involved.

The scissors. Everyone can do the old-fashioned scissors jump. If a whole class is turned loose to jump on the school playground, almost every youngster will use the scissors style and perform easily and naturally.

In photo sequence 23 we get a look at this common and almost instinctive style. In photos 23a and 23b the run is being made. For a left-footed jumper the approach is from the right side of the runway. The take-off (photo 23c) is made from the outside foot. It is easier to spring from the outside foot, because there is much less tendency to lean toward the crossbar. Notice that even our beginner in the photo is quite upright and seems to be getting a solid push against the ground.

Photo 23d shows that the body's center of gravity has actually been driven rather high in the air. But obviously the clearance (photo 23e) is inefficient. With some modification the scissors can be converted into the eastern style, a form that was used widely until the 1930s.

It is clear that the serious candidate cannot stay very long with the scissors. Its inefficient clearance puts too low a ceiling on performance. But

Getting Started

the early scissors jumping is not wasted. It lends itself to a balanced and firm take-off. It is a good way to get the feel of jumping.

The inside foot. Soon after being introduced to jumping by the scissors style, the candidate gets new instructions. He is asked to approach the crossbar from the other side of the runway so that the take-off is made from the inside foot. Instructions are purposely kept very general. Any style will do. He should just jump and not worry about his method of clearance. The typical result produced by such instruction is shown in photo sequence 24. The athlete continues to work with emphasis on a solid feeling of the jumping foot against the ground and the best lift he can get. Efficiency of clearance is ignored.

First straddle effort. The beginner is asked to jump the same way that he did before. Again, he is asked to concentrate on a solid take-off. But now there is one added instruction. At the height of his lift, he is to look at the sky—lift off the ground with a solid drive—then look at the sky. (In photo sequence 25 he is doing this while remaining in place on the ground.)

Photo sequence 26 is particularly interesting because it shows an actual first straddle effort following the above procedure and the simple instructions that were given. The jump is far from perfect, but it does demonstrate that a start can be made rather easily. The candidate now knows that he can do a straddle. The task ahead is to keep improving.

Photo 26d is highly significant. In his first straddle try our beginner is probably performing better than he will for a long time to come. He has fairly good body height, and his clearance brings him almost parallel to the crossbar. The reason for this early performance is simple but highly important. Because he concentrated on his instructions, he was able to keep the lift separate from the roll. What occupied him was the task of first making a solid take-off and then turning his head. Of course, the turning of the head initiates a rotation or roll of the body without the jumper's thinking in terms of roll or clearance. He was busy with his take-off and did that first. It was only afterward that he turned his head.

It might be nice to think that from this point on improvement would be steady. Unfortunately, not so. You must be prepared for temporary setbacks. This is part of the game. Photo sequence 27 shows what actually happens. At a later date, and at an increased height, the candidate is having some problems. Compare with photo sequence 24. Earlier, he was able to carry out a fairly good lift and then roll afterward. Now he is trying to roll as he takes off, and this amounts to a headlong rush toward the pit. He is no longer thinking of lift and turn. He has forgotten the

Getting Started

original instructions. There is a natural anxiety to get by the crossbar, and this anxiety blots out the athlete's image of what he is trying to do. From here on his progress is going to depend largely on the development of clear mental imagery and concentration.

Emphasis on the legs is always important to good performance and a sound take-off, but it becomes particularly important in the early stages, when anxiety to rush at the crossbar interferes with learning. When attention is turned to the legs there is less interest in the crossbar. Working with a tentative checkmark is one effective way to bring attention back to the legs and away from the crossbar. The beginner's first checkmark need only involve a few strides—four strides would be about right for a starter (photo sequence 28).

Obtaining a checkmark is a simple procedure if a few important points are observed. First, in running back from the take-off spot try to use the same speed and rhythm that you intend to use for an actual jump. Second, when you make your approach, try to have full faith in your checkmark. Don't alter your stride when you are actually on the way to the take-off. Once you hit your checkmark, commit yourself. If afterward you find that your mark is bringing you either too close or too far away from the spot that you want to hit, you can then make an adjustment. But, again, make no changes when you are running (photo sequence 29).

Even if you have had little or no previous jumping experience, the chances are that by now you can carry out a style that will at least be recognized as a straddle. You are aware, of course, that there is a long road ahead. Your goal is to make your form increasingly effective and to steadily improve your performance. You are going to do this by developing strength and conditioning, understanding your event, and practicing in an intelligent way. In a later section we will be working on the learning problem.

23. The old-fashioned scissors is a good way to get started. It permits a good lift, but the clearance is inefficient.

23d

23a

23e

23b

23f

23c

24. Approach is from the other side of the bar, so that an inside foot is used for take-off. Instructions are to just jump and not worry about clearance.

24d

24a

24e

24b

24f

24c

25a

25b

25c

25. An added instruction. As before, emphasis is on lift. Lift and then look at the sky.

26. First straddle try. A good jump, because attention is on instructions.

26a

26b

26c

26d

26e

26f

27a

27b

27c

27d

27. Attention is drawn to the crossbar, and the take-off becomes less effective.

28. A simple four-step checkmark is established.

28a

28b

28c

28d

28e

28f

29. The checkmark brings attention back to the legs and improves the take-off.

29a

29b

29c

29d

29e

29f

Your Coach

You may already have a coach, but if not, eventually you will. Your relationship with your coach will be valuable to you in many ways. He will, of course, be most helpful to your jumping achievement, but even more important, he will be a fine influence on your entire life. Today, many prominent and successful people look back with gratitude on their relationships with their coaches. Behind nearly every great athlete there is a skilled and dedicated athletic coach.

In learning the high jump you are basically responsible. It is your career and your life. How well you do will depend primarily on your own determination, your own ambitions. Nevertheless, you need the help of a trained observer. Your coach is in a position to make observations that you cannot. Give him your complete cooperation, and you will progress faster and go farther.

30. A world-record holder works closely with his famous coach.

30a

30b

30c

Learning

The principles of good high jumping are relatively simple. The main task—height, then clearance—should be easy to understand. All of the points of technique relate to the main task, and these points are not difficult to grasp.

Then what seems to be the trouble? Why do so few candidates even approach a mastery of the high jump? Many bright and dedicated young men have devoted their college years to the event without becoming expert. Often they fail to reach anywhere near the performance levels indicated by their aptitudes. Why should this be so?

We don't know all about the reasons why learning the high jump is so difficult and slow. To a certain extent different athletes have different problems. Yet some useful generalizations can be made. First, many candidates for the high jump do not have a clear enough view of their event. They appear to have a sort of blind faith that if they jump regularly things will somehow work out all right. They may work faithfully but blindly. The same errors are repeated day after day, and, as a result, these errors tend to become more and more stamped. The longer an error is carried out, the harder it is to get rid of it.

Many athletes do have a kind of understanding of the high jump. But often such an understanding tends to be only skin deep. It tends to fade away when the showdown comes. The grasp of the event is not really built into the nervous system and the muscles. It disappears when the athlete faces the actual task of clearing the crossbar. This pattern is common enough to be the rule rather than the exception. Your goal must be to avoid this common pattern and make progress. What should you do about it?

First, you must understand the high jump not only with your mind but with your entire system. You have got to feel it. Keep fixing clearly in your mind the main idea of the high jump—height! Understand the "why" of each point of form that makes for greater height. You should not only know that you need a long last stride; you should clearly understand why it is needed. Even that is not enough. You should mentally rehearse the feel of a long last stride, the muscle feel of a solid take-off.

The learning involved in a motor skill like the high jump must be more intense than that of the classroom. It must be very deeply rooted. It has to be a part of you.

If we could look at the mental imagery or mind of the typical high jumper, we would see something pretty much as follows. As he is poised to begin his run, he has a reasonably clear idea of what he intends to do. He may visualize the points of form that he intends to carry out. However, when he begins his approach, his mental image begins to get a little fuzzier. With each stride the image becomes even hazier. By the last stride he draws a blank, forgetting all the things he intended to do. He then makes a blind and anxious rush at the crossbar. An effective jump is out of the question. Learning does not take place. Even worse, the pattern tends to be repeated and hence stamped in.

It is not unusual to see a candidate caught by this trap every practice day for his entire four years. The great psychological obstacle seems to be anxiety to clear the crossbar. This anxiety destroys concentration. It takes attention away from the take-off effort. Were it not for this obstacle almost anyone could jump with reasonable efficiency. Learning to overcome this obstacle is learning to jump itself.

The psychological reality we have been discussing should not give you a gloomy outlook. It should, in fact, make learning the high jump more interesting and challenging. You will be dealing with a fascinating psychological problem. There is no quick or sure-fire solution. Work is going to be necessary.

Learning a motor skill always presents some psychological problems, and that seems to go double for the high jump. We don't have to get concerned about technical terms, but it is useful for us to consider the phrase "conscious control." By these words we mean only that the learner must be able to give clear and conscious attention to the act that he is trying to learn.

In high jumping the most critical act, the one that must be learned, is the one that occurs on the ground—the take-off. And this is the very event that gets blurred by the anxiety to get by the crossbar. The main learning task is to develop a mental attitude that permits the events of the take-off

Learning

to get the cold, clear-eyed attention that they deserve. Many of your drills will be useful in helping you develop a powerful and effective take-off, but you still must practice the take-off under the conditions of a full jump.

Do not hold yourself responsible for making a good take-off. Be realistic and accept the fact that you are not going to carry out the jump correctly for a while. But do make yourself responsible for a *report* on what happened. Make yourself a sharp witness to what you did. Upon the completion of each jump, try to be able to give an accurate description of the take-off events. Be ready to describe such features as the length of your last stride, how solidly you felt over your jumping foot, the position of your body, the swing of your lead leg, etc.

At first you won't find this process of reporting too easy, especially when you try new heights. As the bar is put higher, you will have a tendency to lose your "cool" and rush toward it. This will blur your perception and memory of events. Expect this natural reaction, and don't worry about it. But keep making the effort to report clearly to yourself. You will get better and better at it.

The ability to report well is a highly important first step in learning. It is not going to guarantee you immediate success, but it almost assures you of eventual success. Working in a clear-eyed and systematic manner is bound to speed up your mastery of the high jump.

You've got to *think* about the high jump—off the field as well as on the field. Probably no athlete has ever done well in any athletic event without giving the event lots of thought outside of practice hours. You have to be dedicated to your event. The actual practice sessions on the field are only the formal portion of your work.

As you stand poised to start your run, rehearse. Rehearse what you actually intend to do. Picture the action in your mind's eye. Try to hold this picture during the jump. After you land in the pit, remember what you did. Then, as you walk back from the pit, compare what you did with what you would like to have done.

These mental rehearsals are essential to progress. In the early stages such rehearsals will be made up mostly of a series of mental images. Later on, these rehearsals will be extended to include imagined muscle sensations. In thinking of what you are going to do you will actually feel the jump. When you can do that, you are really on your way.

NOTES

NOTES